THE
LITTLE
CURRY
BOOK

Pat Chapman

PIATKUS

Other titles in the series

The Little Green Avocado Book
The Little Garlic Book
The Little Pepper Book
The Little Apple Book
The Little Strawberry Book
The Little Lemon Book
The Little Bean Book
The Little Nut Book
The Little Mushroom Book
The Little Mustard Book
The Little Rice Book
The Little Honey Book
The Little Tea Book
The Little Coffee Book

© 1985 Judy Piatkus (Publishers) Limited

British Library Cataloguing in Publication Data
Chapman, Pat, *1940–*
The little curry book.
1. Cookery (Curry)
I. Title
641.3'384   TX810.C9

ISBN 0–86188–364–0

Cover and drawings by Hanife Hassan
Designed by Ken Leeder

Typeset by Phoenix Photosetting, Chatham
Printed and bound by The Bath Press

CONTENTS

WHAT IS CURRY?

Curry is unique.
With the word 'curry', taste buds are awakened, mouths water, expectations are aroused and images are evoked. Curry can mean a particular dish, a whole meal, a banquet, a cuisine, a country, indeed a sub-continent. No other style of cooking is summed up so neatly and so completely by a single word.

Curiously, curry has no direct translation into any of India's fifteen languages. It is an English word, although it is now accepted and understood in India. There are a number of theories as to how it came into existence in English. The *Oxford English Dictionary* specifically attributes it to a southern Indian language, Tamil, in the year 1598; *Kari*, pronounced curry, means a type of sauce. There are other candidates for the derivation: *Turkuri* is a seasoned stew from a certain part of India, and *Karhi* is a soup-like dish from the west of India made from spices, chickpea flour dumplings and buttermilk. *Kari phulia* are small leaves called 'curry leaves' used rather like bay leaves. And the *Karahi* or *Karai* is the wok-like frying pan used all over India.

There are many varieties and styles of Indian

cooking. The country is larger than Europe, and is composed of many different races, religions and customs. In the north they prefer lightly spiced meat dishes in thick sauces; in the south they prefer light sauces very highly spiced. Over eighty per cent of Indians are vegetarian, and the climate and therefore the ingredients vary enormously in the different parts of the country. The style of cooking that we in the West prefer is the one developed by the Moghul emperors; creamy, well-spiced meat or poultry dishes. In fact, we enjoy our curries more highly spiced than many northern Indians, a fact borne out by the numerous 'hot' curries invented by restaurateurs in Britain. The Madras curry, or vindaloo, of the High Street Indian restaurant bear little resemblance to those dishes in their place of origin. No one in India has ever heard of phal – the hottest curry on the menu – yet it is highly popular here. However, korma, kofta, keema, rhogan gosht, sag gosht, biriani and pullaos are all authentic Indian curries with which we are familiar.

No one could possibly count how many different curry dishes there are. Every cook who mixes spices and cooks a curry does it in an individual way, and the choice of spices can be quite controversial. Arguments rage between the Gujarati Indian in the west and the Kashmiri in the north, or the Bengali in the east and the Madrassi in the south. Each will have particular ways of doing things, and each will be equally right because curry dishes are as variable and as interesting, and sometimes as unexpected and as different, as wine.

THE HISTORY OF CURRY AND SPICES

In 3000 BC, the three main civilisations, apart from China, were in Egypt, Mesopotamia (which became Persia) and the Harrapan culture in the valley of the river Indus (now Pakistan), which gave its name to India. Each society was literate and was connected by trading routes over land and sea. Oil, textiles, copper and dates went east, whilst ivory and spices came from the Indus. Archaeological remains prove that these spices were used in cooking, in medicine, for beautification and for the embalming of the famous Egyptian mummies.

Tribes of desert-dwelling nomads from Arabia were used to transport the items of trade between the three civilisations and as the civilisations came and went during the next 2,000 years, the Arabs gained the monopoly of the trade routes; in the process they invented the dhow and the caravan, and domesticated the camel.

3

From around 1300 BC, the power of the Greeks began to increase. They traded wine to Egypt and Mesopotamia in return for spices, and by 600 BC it is on record that they used oil, herbs, spices and wine in their cooking. In 327 BC the Greeks invaded India and settled in the Punjab. The Greek empire was now at its peak, and they held a trade monopoly from India to Spain. The Arabs, finding their trading profits somewhat reduced, pioneered new routes by sea to southern India and to the Indonesian islands where they met with Chinese traders and exchanged their goods for Chinese silk and for new and unheard of spices such as nutmeg, mace, cloves, anise and ginger.

At the time of the birth of Christ, the Romans controlled the entire Mediterranean; the Parthians, later Persians, possessed the Greek territories in India and Mesopotamia. The Romans established a trading post at Arikamedu (south of Madras) in India, from where they purchased pepper and muslin and received the spices of the Far East and Indonesia. Chinese silk was brought to the West by a new land route passing north of the Himalayas – known as 'The Silk Route'. The Arabs, however, discovered that if they sailed east to India in the summer and west to Arabia in the winter by using the prevailing monsoon winds, they could halve the journey time and make the crossing non-stop. It was around this time also that a spice route was developed through the Khyber pass from India to the Mediterranean.

In AD 44 Rome captured Britain, and they

brought their spices with them. For the first time England got a taste of garlic, onion, ginger, cassia, saffron, coriander, salt and pepper. All were very valuable, but none more so than the last two. Both were issued as rations to the troops, who promptly used them for barter. Salt was so important that the word 'salary' derives from it, and the phrase 'he's not worth his salt' means that he is not worth paying. Pliny (AD 62–114) described pepper as the most important spice of all, and Apicius, the celebrated Roman gourmet, used it in nearly all his recipes. Pepper was used in place of money at times, and Alaric the Visigoth demanded 3,000 lbs as part of the payment he required to lift his blockade of Rome in 408. Not long after that, the Romans left Britain and the use of spice was forgotten.

When Rome finally collapsed in around 800 the Arabs took over their lands from Spain to India, and once again were in control of the spice routes. Venice found itself a beneficiary of the decline of Rome, being at the head of a route, and the Venetians soon established themselves as the masters of the Mediterranean. Genoa, on the other side of Italy, soon followed suit as a rival. For more than 700 years the Arabs and the Italians made immense fortunes by charging whatever prices they liked for their precious spices.

It was not until 1066 that spices made their reappearance in Britain; the Normans delighted in spicy cooking. Shortly after this, the Arabs came across sugar cane in India and citrus fruits in Indo-China. London became the sugar and spice centre of

England, and fortunes were made by the English merchants and chapmen – the men who sold on the cheap! Pepper continued to be the most precious

spice: in 1200, one pound of pepper would fetch as much as six sheep! Foreign ships entering London paid a levy of pepper, and it was a recognised form of paying due debts, such as (pepper-corn) rent.

Spice prices continued to rise until Tudor times. By then, Spain and Portugal controlled the European Atlantic. Portugal used Antwerp as a base and sent its spice ships to England in competition with the Italian land route. However, by the time the Portuguese had added their margin of profit, the spices they carried were even more expensive than those from Italy. It was time for England to do something. She attempted to become a spice trader. In one abortive attempt, in 1458, a vessel sailed by Robert Sturmy was allowed to collect a cargo of spices from Cairo, but was sunk with all hands by the Genoese off Malta.

Desperate to gain a foot-hold in the lucrative spice and trading markets, England and other northern European countries needed to find new routes to the East. Between 1487 and 1520, Spanish and Portuguese sailors pioneered routes to India, discovered the Americas inadvertently, and reached the Indonesian islands by travelling west. Britain proved herself in 1579 when Drake sailed around the world, then, with growing confidence, he defeated the Spanish Armada in 1588 in a move which gave England, Holland and France the freedom of their own seas. In 1595, the Dutch sailed to the East Indies to capture the clove, nutmeg and mace trade. In 1608, the English reached India and received the permission of the Moghul emperors to trade in direct competition with the Portuguese who had already been there for a hundred years.

The Moghuls had invaded India in 1483 and had quickly established themselves as the most powerful and wealthy rulers India had ever known. Their courts were highly civilised, if at times quite violent, and it was during the time of Moghuls that cooking with spices was taken to great heights. There is plentiful evidence to show that spicy cooking had survived the collapse first of the Harrapans and later of the Greeks. Techniques were passed from generation to generation by word of mouth, and the style of cooking we now know as 'curry' spread all over the Indian peninsula. The Moghuls simply did to their cooking what they did to their architecture, their warfare and their lifestyle . . . they perfected it. Moghul dishes such as biriani, tandoori, pullaos, korma, rhogan gosht and numerous others have not been bettered since. The chefs of the day were given status, time and money to work at their craft. All this was observed, then enjoyed by the early English traders.

Perversely, however, in England a marked change of taste was taking place at exactly this time. It was the time of Cromwell and the Puritans, who in twelve short years in the mid 1600s managed to outlaw anything to do with pleasure and enjoyment. Everything had to be bland and constrained, from dress to revelry, and from attitudes to cuisine. Laws were passed to ensure it. To this day, it is illegal to consume mince pies on Christmas day; Cromwell's law was never repealed. Meat was by then of better quality and new farming methods ensured that it was available throughout the year. Prior to that meat had been seasonal, as surplus cattle were killed off before the winter crop shortage and techniques such as air drying and smoking, along with heavy spicing, were needed to make meat palatable for the long winter months. Also, sugar had made its appearance. It was, by then, cheap enough to be used by everybody, and it made bland and bitter food taste better. England had begun to develop its sweet tooth.

During the eighteenth century pickles and sauces containing spicy mixtures became the vogue. Many recipes for home-made products exist in the cookery books of the time, and several have survived as familiar proprietary brands. The spiciest survivor is Worcestershire sauce, but Branston pickle, pica-lilly, 'brown' sauce, tomato ketchup, anchovy essence and mango chutney were well known then – and all originated in India. Spice mixtures and curry powders also arrived in England in the late 1700s, brought back by the English traders.

CURRY IN BRITAIN

For over three hundred years, until independence was granted in 1947, British men and women had been travelling from England to India and returning, after a lifetime's service, with a taste for all things Indian, including a delight for the food. For most of them Indian food became a memory; there were very few Indian restaurants, and the individual spices were hard to obtain.

Despite the attempts of many generations of memsahibs to capture the flavour of India by bringing back their chefs' mixtures of spices – curry powder – the art of curry-making was never mastered here. What evolved was a revolting stew, thickened with flour, to which was added curry powder and miscellaneous left-overs, raisins, sultanas and apples. It prevailed in works canteens, schools and restaurants for too long.

The shortage of labour in British hospital and transport systems in the 1950s led to a call to Commonwealth countries to supply workers. There was an immediate response from the West Indies and from India and Pakistan. New communities were established in several British cities, and with them came a supportive infra-structure. It was not long before Indian restaurants began to appear in every town.

Within two decades, the trade had expanded. Indian restaurants were no longer relegated to back streets, they were occupying prime High Street sites. They were fashionable, respectable and stylish, and serving high-quality Indian-style food in a market worth over £170 million a year. Curry is now Britain's favourite dining-out food. There are, it is estimated, more Indian-style restaurants in Britain (some 3,500) than anywhere else in the world.

CURRY AROUND THE WORLD

Curry is the indigenous food of more than a quarter of the world's population. It is not just the 700 million residents of India who are curry-eaters; all India's neighbours subsist on curry. Pakistan, Nepal, Bangladesh, Sri Lanka and Burma are all curry lands, and curry also forms an important part of the diet in Thailand, Indonesia and Malaya.

Laos, Vietnam and Cambodia owe their origins to China, where curry does not exist in the form we recognise, although food is spiced with ginger, pepper and some aromatic spices. In Western

China, which shares part of its boundary with Burma, the food is spiced with garlic, ginger, Szechwan pepper and both hot and aromatic spices. In the other regions of China, spicing is limited to such delicate aromatics as star anise and fennel.

As one comes West through the Khyber Pass into Afghanistan, one finds birianis, pullaos, spicy kebabs and curries are the norm. And derivatives of curry are to be found in Iran, Israel, the Arab lands, Turkey and North and East Africa, where very spicy dishes are eaten. Even in Spain one can find direct evidence of Indian influence, spread by the Moorish Arabs during the thirteenth century in the form of paella, which like Turkey's pillaf, descends from pullao.

Indian-style restaurants are rapidly catching on in Australia, New Zealand, and Canada, and especially in the United States. This is not the case in Europe or Latin America, where very few curry restaurants have been established.

SPICY FACTS

THE INDIANS

* The cow is sacred to the Hindus. This probably came about when in 1500 BC India was invaded by the Ayrians, who were cattle farmers. The cow was valuable enough to be used as payment for major transactions. This passed into religious dogma, and today the devout Hindu does not eat beef or veal, which is why you do not find beef curries in Hindu-run restaurants.

* A Moslem does not eat pork. This is because the pig, and other cloven-hooved animals, are considered unclean. Both religions – Hinduism and Islam – permit the consumption of mutton, lamb and poultry.

* The principal religion of India is Hinduism (500m); second is Islam (80m). There are fifteen other religions including Sikhism (9m), Buddhism (6m), Jainism (2m), Christianity (2m) and the Zoroastrian religion (Parsee) (0.1m).

* Jains are total vegetarians. They believe everything has a soul, and believe in non violence. They wear face masks to prevent the inadvertent inhalation and thus killing of small insects. Over 80% of Indians are vegetarian.

* Harems were the invention of the Moslem world. They were a measure of the status and prestige of their 'owners'. The largest were owned by the Moghul emperors and contained not only the most beautiful and desirable women in the land, but women of all skills, from dancers to painters, needlewomen to flower arrangers. Cooking, however, was entrusted only to men.

* Most Indians eat with their right hand. In the north it is considered impolite to allow food to pass the first knuckles, whilst in the south the custom is to use the whole hand.

* A Persian Shah was celebrated for saying that eating with a knife and fork was like making love through an interpreter.

THE BRITISH

* In recognition of the fact that she was now Empress of India, Queen Victoria, in 1887, appointed an Indian to be her 'groom of the chamber', a very personal role. Appointed initially to teach the Queen Hindustani, he was soon seldom out of her sight, and became privy to Her Majesty's state boxes and private thoughts. She gave him the affectionate title of 'Munshi' (teacher) and he later became known as her Indian secretary. This state of affairs was un-nerving to the politicians of the day, and the Queen was obliged to stop showing Karim state secrets. Apart from Hindi, which the Queen never mastered, he did give her and the Royal family a taste for curry, with the meals he cooked on occasion.

* Many Indian restaurants in Britain are called the 'Taj Mahal'. This is probably because their owners felt sure that Westerners would be likely to know the world's most famous building. It was built by the emperor Shah Jahan, as a memorial and tomb for his wife, Mumtaz. It was completed in 1648 and is located in Agra.

* In 1984, Britain consumed £26 million-worth of dried herbs and spices compared with £5.4 million in 1974. Best sellers in 1984 were ginger, pepper, chilli and garlic. In 1974 they were parsley, thyme and sage.

THE FOOD

* Yoghurt is widely used in curry cooking. The origins of yoghurt can be traced back to the Egyptians, and it is probable that it originated more than 5,000 years ago.

* Ice used to be brought down from the slopes of the Himalayas by teams of runners to make ice-cream (kulfi) and yoghurt drink (lhassi) for the emperors when they were in residence in Kashmir.

* The Portuguese were in India from 1498 to 1962, a total of 464 years (as opposed to the British 339 years: 1608 to 1947). Their capital was Goa, and the food of Goa is very different from elsewhere in India. Pork is widely eaten, and the best known

dish is vindaloo, traditionally a very hot pork curry, marinated in vinegar.

* The most popular Indian chutney, mango chutney, was known in Britain by 1750. Such sauces were made popular and given respectability by giving them military brand names such as 'Major Grey's Mango Chutney'.

* A few centuries ago a celebrated feast dish was served to Indian royals. An ox was stuffed with a goat which was stuffed with a rabbit or hare, stuffed with a peahen, stuffed with a quail which was finally stuffed with a finch. Each animal was de-boned in one piece, then marinated in a different spice sauce, and finally roasted. To serve it was sliced crossways.

* 'There is no better breakfast in the world than chupattis spread with coriander chutney and honey syrup and eaten in the early sunshine to the call of doves and barbets.' Tom Stobart, author and Everest climber.

THE SPICES

* Before merchants started moving spices from land to land, they were confined to single areas of wild growth. Native to India was curry leaf, cinnamon, pepper, cardamom, garlic, onion and coriander. Cassia and mango came from Burma. Cloves originated in the Indonesian Moluccan islands of Ternate and Tidore, and nutmeg and

mace came from the tiny nearby island of Ambon. Ginger, lemon grass and turmeric probably came from Borneo. Mustard, fennel and a different species of onion originated in the Near East. Cummin originated in Persia. Chillis, a newcomer to the spice scene, originated in Brazil and the North East of Latin America. They were discovered only 500 years ago.

* A clove is the unopened bud of a flower. It is the world's second most important spice, and earns India some £20 million a year in exports. It takes 8–10,000 cloves to make 1 kilogram.

* 'Heat' in spices comes mainly from chilli peppers, of which there are hundreds of species, varying greatly in 'hotness'. It is also found in peppercorns, and to a lesser extent in ginger and onion, and from other spices.

* Chilli 'burns' the tongue but lessens the taste of sour and bitter; ginger burns the throat and black pepper inhibits all tastes. The best way to counteract heat if you are suffering is to sip a quantity of milk or plain yoghurt. Water does not help.

* Many spices are poisonous if taken in large doses, including saffron, cloves and chilli, but in the small amounts used in cooking there is no danger.

OTHER USES

* Spicy food activates the digestive juices and can in some cases cause indigestion. An antidote to this problem was developed centuries ago in India. It is called pan. Pan is the leaf of the areca or betel nut tree, which grows all over Asia. The leaf is used as the edible outer wrapper of various bitter, sour or sweet ingredients which are mixed according to the eater's taste. Called supari, these ingredients include shredded betel nut, tobacco, cardamom, clove, fennel seed, aniseed, chopped date, coconut, seeds of pumpkin, cucumber and marrow and lime paste.

* Spices have many uses in medicine. Garlic and cloves are used as anti-bacterial and antiseptic agents. A clove is well known by the dentist, as it can be used to diminish the pain of toothache, and for mouth ulcers. Cassia is used to counter nausea and diarrhoea, as is cummin – the latter is used to reduce vomiting during pregnancy, and to increase lactation. Turmeric relieves catarrh, and is an anti-oxidant. Chilli has limited medical use but is anti-bacterial, an efficient digestive aid, and will make the heart beat faster.

* The ancient Egyptians used whole spices and the oils of spices to embalm the bodies of their dead. Cloves, cinnamon and cardamoms were used whole, but steeped in oil, and were packed tightly in the body cavities. Oils were rubbed into the

flesh, and turmeric was used to give the body a golden glow. Many types of whole spices, nuts and fruit were deposited alongside the body and in the tomb for the journey to the next world.

* An aphrodisiac is a comestible which is said to stimulate sexual drive. Spices with this attribute include cardamom, cinnamon, clove, fennel and garlic.

* *To increase potency:*
Shelled black sesame seeds steeped
In the yolk of sparrows' eggs
And ground with waterchestnut, nut grass,
Cowhage, wheat and gram into milky
Honey-sweetened porridge are very efficacious.
        From the Kama Sutra, written c. AD 400
                in Sanskrit, translated by Indra Sinha

* The robes of Bhuddist monks achieve their bright yellow colour because they are dyed in saffron dye. A much cheaper alternative is turmeric, although the results are never as bright.

CURRY HERBS AND SPICES

Although there are literally dozens of spices used in Indian cookery, the recipes in this book use no more than 24, and of those only twelve are 'essential'.

THE BIG FIVE SPICES

CHILLI: Chillies are used whole, fresh or dried, or ground. They are used specifically to add heat to a dish. There are only four species of chilli, but from them grow thousands of sub-species, including the capsicum. The endless varieties vary in shape from cherry to cucumber; in colour from green to white, yellow, orange, red and purple; in texture from fleshy to scaly; and in taste from sweet and mild to incendiary hot. Hottest are the tiny 'bird' or Tabasco chilli.

CORIANDER: Used whole or ground, for sweetness. The seeds are whitish brown and are 2 – 3 mm in diameter. India produces over 80,000 tonnes a year, and most goes overseas. The leaves are used fresh as a herb.

CUMMIN: Used whole or ground, these seeds give a savoury taste to the dish. They are yellow-brown, about 4mm long, and used extensively in curry cooking.

PAPRIKA: This is the ground powder of the red capsicum. It is not hot and is used principally for colouring a curry. Paprika is the Hungarian name for pepper, and it was they who made it synonymous with their native dish. Who has not relished a Hungarian goulash, so generously coloured by paprika? Today there is a thriving paprika industry in California, as well as in Spain and Eastern Europe, and it has also found its way to India, and into curry.

TURMERIC: Used in ground, powdered form, turmeric gives curry its distinctive yellow colour. Turmeric is a rhizome related to the ginger plant. It grows all over South Asia. When the root is dug from the earth it is then boiled for up to an hour, drained and dried in the sun for two weeks until it is dry and hard. It is then cleaned and ground into the familiar yellow powder.

AROMATICS

BAY LEAVES: These aromatic leaves are used in garam masala, as a substitute for cassia leaves which are almost impossible to get in the West. Bay does grow in India, but is relatively little used.

CARDAMOMS:
Green or white: These small pods are known in India as the 'Queen of Spices'. Their delicate taste is enjoyed in savoury and sweet cooking; raw, they aid digestion and sweeten the breath. They are one of the world's most expensive spices.
Brown or black: These seeds are two or three times the size of the green cardamom and have a rather more pungent, though still aromatic, fragrance. They are used ground in garam masala, and whole in some dishes.

CASSIA BARK: Cassia is the bark of a type of cinnamon tree. It is corkier and thicker than true cinnamon, which is harvested in parchment-thin quills. Cassia has an aromatic, pleasant sweet fragrance, which is used whole in certain dishes and in ground garam masala.

CLOVES: If ever there was a spice over which wars were fought, the clove is it. It is one of the few spices which remained in use in England after the Reformation. Even today it remains, after pepper, the world's second most important spice, coming principally these days from Zanzibar.

FENNEL SEEDS: These sweet seeds are widely used in all Mediterranean cooking, but a bit less so in Indian. The greenish-yellow seeds grow to around 4–5mm and are used in the more delicately flavoured dishes.

BLACK PEPPER: Black pepper is known in India as the 'King of Spices'. It is India's biggest spice revenue earner. Pepper is used in every country on earth. Peppercorns are the fruit or berries of the pepper vine, which grows only in monsoon forests. The fruit berries, or spikes, are first green, changing colour through yellow to orange-red when ripe. Depending on the colour of the spikes when cropped, you will get green, black or white peppercorns, for they are all one and the same thing. Green peppercorns are very immature, and are either bottled immediately in order to retain their colour, or they are air-dried. To obtain black peppercorns, the spikes are picked when they start changing colour to yellow. They are dried in the sun and become black and shrivelled. To harvest white pepper, the spikes are left on the vines until they turn red. The outer red skin is removed at once, revealing an inner white berry which is then dried out. Pink pepper is obtained the same way from a particular variety, and air-dried to prevent it turning white.

SOME OTHER SPICES

Each of the following ten spices has a particular characteristic which makes it important for one dish or another.

ASAFOETIDA: This originates as the gum or sticky sap of a tree. It crystallises and is then ground to powder. How it ever came to be used as a spice we shall never know because it smells like old socks or worse. Used in small quantities its function is to minimise 'fishy tastes'. It also aids digestion by reducing flatulence and is used in dishes containing lentils and beans.

CURRY LEAVES: These are the leaves of the neem tree. In several Indian languages they are known as Kari leaves. They are much used in South Indian cooking, because the tree is indigenous to that area. The leaves can be used fresh or dry. They do not taste of curry – instead they are rather lemony.

FENUGREEK SEEDS: These golden seeds of the fenugreek plant are quite widely used in Indian cooking – especially in branded curry powders. They are extremely bitter and should therefore be treated with respect.

LEMON GRASS: These are blades of a particular species of grass. They appear in the cooking of the countries further east than India. The blades should give off a delightfully fragrant lemony smell. Use fresh or dried.

MANGO POWDER: Literally, the powder of dried mangoes. This is very sour and is used sparingly in place of vinegar or lemon juice.

MUSTARD SEEDS: These little black seeds are very popular in South Indian cooking. They are hottish and add interest to dishes such as lemon rice.

SAFFRON: Saffron is the world's most expensive spice, reflecting not scarcity but the extraordinary amount of labour required to crop it. It is the golden stamen of a variety of crocus. Only three grow to each crocus, and it requires 70,000 individual crocuses, or 200,000 stamen, to make one pound of saffron. At over £1,000 per pound, it is indeed valuable. Fortunately only a quarter of a gram is sufficient to impart a wonderful flavour and fragrance to kormas, rice or some desserts.

SESAME SEEDS: Neutral in taste and used for texture in delicate cooking. They are used in kormas and with onion seeds as a coating on nan bread.

STAR ANISE: A lovely shape and a familiar sweet taste to those who frequent their local confectioner. It appears in Chinese cooking more than in Indian.

WILD ONION SEEDS: Bitter-tasting on their own, these jet black, tiny nuggets become transformed when cooked. The most popular use is as a coating with sesame seeds on nan bread.

ROOTS AND BULBS

Indian cookery makes extensive use of two roots or rhizomes: turmeric, already described, and ginger, and also of two bulbs: garlic and onion.

GINGER: The best grade of ginger is one with three or more 'fingers'. Fresh ginger has become widely known in the West. It travels well and lasts for a long time after being cropped. It can also be dried in the sun and ground.

GARLIC: The bulb grows underground and consists of six to thirty cloves, each covered in a thin whitish-pink papery skin, which must be removed before cooking. Garlic is readily available fresh, but it can be obtained in powder form, which is totally acceptable in Indian cooking, but which gives a different flavour to fresh garlic.

ONION: The onion's single underground bulb varies in size and strength of flavour and heat depending on the variety, of which there are hundreds. The type used in India has a bright pink skin, not unlike the French type, and is quite potent. The Spanish onion is large and relatively bland, whilst the English onion, with its golden-orange skin rates somewhere in between. All are acceptable for curry cooking.

HERBS

Compared with many styles of cooking, herbs do not figure largely in Indian cookery. These are the three which do:

FRESH CORIANDER: This is the most used. Easy to grow and cheap, coriander is a variety of parsley. It is now becoming widely available from the greengrocer and grows throughout the year.

MINT: Seasonal, but can be obtained bottled. Avoid bright green bottled jellies.

FENUGREEK: A very savoury-tasting leaf, it is quite acceptable to use in dry form from packets.

STORING SPICES

Whole spices should keep for many years if they were dried properly in the sun after being cropped, but it is better to buy them to use within months rather than years.

Ground spices are made from whole spices and the action of grinding 'atomises' the spice and at once small particles are released into the air. It is these that you can smell, but the fragrant oils soon disperse and you are left with a relatively tasteless odourless powder.

Factory-ground spices are sealed in bags as fast as possible, and it is not until you open the bag that you 'start the clock'. Do not leave ground spices lying around in opened packets: keep them in airtight jars or bottles for three to four months. After that they will slowly lose their quality, eventually becoming tasteless.

Neither ground nor whole spices should be kept in direct sunlight. They fade rapidly, particularly ground spices, and look unappetising. Keep them in the dark, in containers, and plan your store quantities carefully.

USING SPICES

There is an enormous amount of flexibility when it comes to choosing which spices to use for a particular recipe. It is less confusing to the taste buds to use a few spices rather than too many. It is the overall appearance of the dish that matters. For example, rhogan gosht (page 38) should have a predominantly red look and taste quite aromatic; yellow spices are avoided and aromatics are used rather than savoury spices. Sag gosht (page 40), on the other hand, is savoury and green, so red spices are omitted and yellow are used. To obtain a white curry (korma, page 44), the spicing is minimal and red and yellow are avoided.

Spicing is a form of seasoning, on a grander scale, and it is a very personal matter. Some people prefer a bit more heat, or a bit less savoury taste, or more sweet, so experiment to your own taste.

All spices start their commercial lives whole. Some are used whole in particular recipes, particularly the aromatic spices, and others are ground. Whole spices release their flavour slowly during the entire cooking process; ground spices can be made into a paste which blends and cooks better.

GRINDING SPICES

With three exceptions – chilli, turmeric and ginger – it is always better to grind your own spices. You will get the best fragrance and quality, there will be no adulterative husks or stalks in your own mix, and it will be fresh. You can use a mortar and pestle to do the job the traditional and hard way, but for a small investment it is much easier to use an electric coffee grinder. It can still be used for coffee, of course – just unplug and wipe clean. Grind exactly the amount you need for the day's cooking.

PREPARING SPICES

Before spices can be used in curry cooking there is work to do. Spices are seeds. They are raw, having at most been dried in the hot sun immediately after being harvested. Even ground spices are raw and simply spooning spices into a bubbling pot will not remove the 'green' taste. To do this, spices must either be roasted or fried. In both cases one is aiming to remove moisture content without searing out the essential oils. In either case the spices must not be burnt. If they are, the carbon taste will remain with the dish throughout. If you burn the spices throw them away and start again.

As with coffee, the aroma which roasting gives off is wonderful. You can use an oven (160°C/325°F/ Gas 3) for 10 minutes, or a dry pan on the stove at medium heat or the grill pan at half heat and not too close to the heating element for the same length of time. A good roasting exercise is to do a batch of garam masala. Roast in bulk and store the spare.

GARAM MASALA

Literally meaning 'hot spice mix', garam masala is a combination of aromatic and hot spices which are used to enliven a curry at its last stages. Add it and cook for a few minutes in order not to lose the subtlety of the aromatics. There are many recipes for garam masala. This one is prepared in two stages so that you can add the heat to the aromatics only if you wish to. It will yield about 3½ oz or 100 g.

SPICES 1

Coriander seeds	27 g	(5 teaspoons)
Cummin seeds	27 g	(5 teaspoons)
Cassia bark	8 g	(1 teaspoon)
Cloves	8 g	(1½ teaspoons)
Cardamoms: black/brown	8 g	(3 or 4 large pods)
Nutmeg	4g	(1 teaspoon, ground)
Bay leaves	2½ g	(3 or 4 leaves)

SPICES 2

Black pepper, ground	12 g	(2–3 teaspoons)
Ginger powder	4 g	(1 teaspoon)

Preheat oven to 160°C/325°F/Gas 3, or the grill or a ring on the stove to medium.

Meanwhile, weigh out SPICES 1 into the oven pan or dry frying pan. Heat the spices in the oven for 10 minutes, or under the grill or on the stove until lightly browned. If they burn, throw them out and start again.

Cool the spices, then grind in a coffee grinder, small amounts at a time.

Mix in SPICES 2. If you prefer aromatics without heat, omit SPICES 2.

Store in a jar or container. Use as directed in recipes.

SPICE PASTES AND PURÉES

FRYING THE SPICE PASTE

This is a very important part of cooking successful curries. Most of the recipes in this book require you to make a paste of the listed ground spices. Use a few drops of water or stock, or, in a robust curry, vinegar, and make the paste to a dropping consistency, i.e. not at all runny. Leave the paste for a few minutes to enable the spice powder to soak up the liquid. Re-adjust the liquid content if it has gone too stiff, and continue as directed in the recipe, or as follows:

While it is standing, heat up two tablespoons oil in a frying pan. It should be quite hot. Carefully put the paste into the pan (it may splutter) and fry for about two minutes, stirring very frequently. It is ready when the liquid has evaporated and the oil separates. Remove from the heat.

It is possible to fry the powder without making a paste, but the purpose of the paste is to saturate the powder in liquid which protects it from instant burning. A paste also results in a better texture.

PURÉES

A purée is equally important. It helps you get the right texture to your curry throughout its cooking.

Your purée will be onion, either on its own or with ginger and garlic. You may add or subtract any of these ingredients to your taste. Onion is used because it is relatively neutral in taste, but in purée form it provides an ideal base to prevent the fried spice paste from becoming overcooked. Garlic adds savoury taste, and after prolonged cooking it does not taint the breath. Ginger adds a distinctive hot taste which blends in when well cooked. They can be puréed separately and added during the cooking.

To make the purée:
Peel and coarsely chop onion – or garlic or ginger. One large onion will make approximately 5 fl oz (150 ml) purée, or enough to fill a small yoghurt pot.

Heat some oil in a frying pan. Don't be sparing unless you are on a diet. Fry the chopped onion on a low to medium heat. When you want to use it, strain off the spare oil and purée.

If you have a food processor, making a purée takes a few seconds. A blender usually requires you to add a little water to obtain the purée (and this would have to be strained or cooked out). The hardest way to make purée is to mash everything through a strainer: it's messy and time-consuming.

Tip: Make a relatively large amount of purée. Put the excess into individual small yoghurt pots, measured out for future recipes, and freeze.

CURRY RECIPES

HOT CURRY, 'MADRAS' STYLE

This is a restaurant favourite (although not the hottest) and it can be made from chicken, turkey, lamb or beef. Adding pepper and chilli to taste, the tomato and ground almonds add a counter-balancing and distinctive flavour.

1½ lb (680 g) meat or poultry
4–5 tablespoons vegetable oil or ghee
5 fl oz (150 ml) onion purée (see page 33)
14 oz (400 g) tin tomatoes, strained
2 tablespoons ground almonds
2 tablespoons tomato purée
Salt to taste

SPICES 1
2 cardamom pods, green or white
4 dry red chillies
½ teaspoon chilli powder
1 teaspoon white cummin seeds
1 teaspoon fenugreek seeds
½ teaspoon ground black pepper
1 teaspoon turmeric

SPICES 2
1 dessertspoon dry fenugreek leaves
1 dessertspoon garam masala

Remove fat or skin from beef or lamb, and cut in 1 inch (2.5 cm) cubes. Poultry can be left on the bone if liked. Fry in oil or ghee for about 10 minutes, then strain the oil back into the pan.

Fry the onion purée in the same oil for 5–8 minutes, then add SPICES 1, cooking for a further 5 minutes. Add the tinned tomatoes, almonds and tomato purée and mix well.

Put into a casserole in a preheated oven (at 190°C/375°/Gas 5) and cook for 45–60 minutes. Stir halfway through the cooking time and add a little water if the curry is drying up.

Then add SPICES 2 and salt. Mix and return to the oven for 10 minutes.

Serves 4

'We dine at 2 o'clock in the very heat of the day . . . A soup, a roast fowl, curry and rice, a mutton pie, a forequarter of lamb, a rice pudding, tarts, very good cheese, fresh churned butter and excellent Madeira. (That is very expensive but the eatables are cheap.)'

Quoted by a Mrs Fay in Calcutta in 1780

VEGETABLE BHAJEE

This curry has a total absence of 'heat'.

10 oz (300 g) potatoes
4 oz (115 g) carrots
4 oz (115 g) turnips (if available)
3 tablespoons vegetable oil or ghee
8 fl oz (200 g) onion purée (see page 33)
4 oz (115 g) tomatoes, tinned or fresh
4 oz (115 g) peas
Salt to taste

SPICES
1 teaspoon ground coriander
1 teaspoon ground cummin
2 teaspoons garlic powder
2 teaspoons paprika
1 teaspoon turmeric

Wash, peel and chop the potatoes, carrots and turnips, then blanch in boiling water for about 5 minutes. Strain.

Mix the SPICES with a little water to form a stiffish paste.

Heat the oil, fry the onion purée until hot, then add the spice paste. Fry for 5 minutes or so, stirring frequently.

Combine blanched vegetables with the fried onion and spices, then add the tomatoes and peas.

Simmer until cooked — about 15–20 minutes – adding salt to taste.

Serves 4

A GREAT FEAST OF KING DASARATHA

'Beautiful white mansions were erected, with stables for elephants and horses. Palaces with their balconies decorated with leaves and flowers were to be seen, and others adorned with green and flowery sprays and garlands of pure white blossoms sprinkled with scented water. These dwellings contained square courts serving as reception halls with space for palaquins, and coaches. Food of all kinds, hot rice in heaps as high as mountains, curry and other fare combining all tastes, was to be found there, with sugar-cane, every variety of confection, pancakes and other delicious dishes served in clean vessels, while excellent couches with spotless coverings and quilts were spread for relaxation.'

From the Ramayana and the Mahabarata, Hindu epic poems written around 1000–300 BC

RED CURRY: RHOGAN JOSH GOSHT

Literally meaning lamb in red sauce, this dish derives from the times of the Moghul emperors and is aromatic and tasty. The red colour is enhanced by red meat, tomato and paprika. For more dramatic effect, add cochineal or red food colouring as directed in the recipe.

1½ lb (680 g) lean lamb, cubed
5 fl oz (150 ml) yoghurt
1 teaspoon salt
8 fl oz (200 g) onion purée (see page 33)
1 tablespoon ginger purée (see page 33)
2 teaspoons garlic purée (see page 33)
4–5 tablespoons vegetable oil or ghee
6 fresh tomatoes, puréed
1 tablespoon chopped fresh coriander (if available)
Salt to taste

SPICES 1
3 green cardamoms
3 small pieces cassia bark
½ teaspoon chilli powder
3 cloves
1 teaspoon ground coriander
1 teaspoon ground cummin

SPICES 2
1 dessertspoon garam masala
3 teaspoons paprika
⅛ teaspoon red food colouring powder (optional)

Mix together the lamb, yoghurt, SPICES 1 and 1 teaspoon salt. Let stand for 6 hours minimum, or overnight, to allow the flavours to marinate well.

Fry the onion, ginger and garlic purées in the oil for 5–8 minutes, then add the tomato and fry for a further 3 or 4 minutes.

Put the meat mixture and the fried purées into an oven casserole dish. Place in a preheated oven (190°C/375°F/Gas 5) and cook for about 45 minutes. Stir about halfway through, adding water if necessary.

Add SPICES 2, fresh coriander and salt. Mix well and cook for a further 10–15 minutes, then serve.

Serves 4

'March to barracks where with joy
Their masticators they employ.
O curry, rice and beef and goat,
voraciously they cram each throat.'

An unknown author about the
Indian army, late eighteenth century

GREEN CURRY: SAAG GOSHT

Gosht means lamb in Hindi and Saag (or Sag) means spinach. The combination of lamb in puréed spinach will give you a rich, creamy-textured green curry, provided only yellow and brown spices are used. The result is a really pleasant savoury taste.

1½ lb (680 g) lean lamb
4–5 tablespoons vegetable oil or ghee
5 fl oz (150 ml) onion purée (see page 33)
2 teaspoons ginger purée (see page 33)
2 teaspoons garlic purée (see page 33)
1 tablespoon vinegar
4 fresh tomatoes, chopped
1 lb (450 g) spinach, washed and puréed
4 tablespoons chopped fresh coriander
Salt to taste

SPICES 1
2 cardamoms brown/black
4 cloves
1 teaspoon cummin seeds

SPICES 2
½ teaspoon chilli powder
½ teaspoon ground coriander
½ teaspoon ground black pepper
½ teaspoon turmeric

SPICES 3
1 dessertspoon dry fenugreek leaves
1 teaspoon garam masala

Remove any fat from the meat and cut into cubes. Fry in the oil for 5–10 minutes. Strain off the oil into the pan and put the meat on one side.

Heat the same oil and fry SPICES 1. Add the purées and stir-fry for 5–8 minutes.

Make a paste of SPICES 2 with the vinegar. Add it to the purée. Fry for a further 5 minutes.

Combine the meat, purée, tomatoes and the spinach (no need to blanche it) in a casserole dish, mixing well. Cook in a preheated oven (190°C/375°F/Gas 5) for 45–60 minutes. Stir during cooking, adding water if necessary.

Then add SPICES 3, fresh coriander and salt, and cook for at least another 10 minutes.

Serves 4

YELLOW CURRY: PRAWN MOLLEE

The end result here is a light, bright yellow curry. I've chosen prawns, but you could use any fish or shellfish or even chicken breast to achieve the same result. The key spice is turmeric, and if you feel affluent add a little saffron. The whiteness of the coconut adds brightness to the finished curry.

2 teaspoons wine vinegar
1 large onion, chopped
1 clove garlic, finely chopped
2 tablespoons mustard or sunflower oil
3 fl oz (75 ml) coconut milk (if available)
1½ lb (680 g) prawns (thawed and strained if frozen)
2 green chillies, chopped (optional)
1 tablespoon coconut (fresh and chopped, or desiccated)
Milk
Salt to taste
Lemon juice

SPICES
¼ teaspoon asafoetida
½ teaspoon ground ginger
2 black peppercorns
½ teaspoon turmeric
½ teaspoon saffron strands (optional)

Make a paste of the SPICES and the vinegar, plus water if needed.

Fry the onion and garlic in the oil until golden. Add the spice paste and the coconut milk (or water).

When hot, add the prawns with the chillies (if used) and coconut. Keep the sauce fairly liquid while cooking by adding milk as required. Cook for 10–15 minutes or so until the fish is tender. Add salt to taste. As soon as cooked, sprinkle with lemon juice, and serve with plain rice and accompaniments.

If you wish to use saffron, soak it in a tablespoon of warm milk for a few minutes then add it to the fish just before serving.

Serves 4

'One should not talk with food in mouth;
One should not throw food in mouth;
One should not stuff his mouth full of food;
One should not shake one's hands when eating as
one would scatter rice all over, because the fingers
are used;
One should not put one's tongue out when eating;
One should not make hissing sounds when eating;
One should not lick one's finger, bowl or accept
drinking cup with hands which are soiled with food;
Everyone should start eating at the same time.'

'An etiquette for Buddhist Monks',
from the writings of Buddha, c. 600 BC

WHITE CURRY: CHICKEN KORMA

It seems unlikely – a white curry – but the use of yoghurt, cream, white cashew nuts and light coloured spices and chicken breast will achieve a most delicately spiced pale curry. Kormas were another favourite of the Moghuls. A delicious vegetarian dish can be made by substituting 1 lb (450 g) cauliflower and 8 oz (225 g) peas for the chicken.

1½ lb (680 g) chicken (skinned, off the bone)
3 oz (75 g) cashew nuts or almonds (or mixture)
2 teaspoons ginger purée (see page 33)
1 teaspoon garlic purée (see page 33)
2 green chillies, finely chopped (optional)
3 fl oz (75 ml) yoghurt
1 cup vegetable oil or ghee
1 medium onion, chopped
3 fl oz (75 ml) double cream
Salt to taste
3 tablespoons chopped fresh coriander or parsley (if available)

SPICES 1
2 whole green cardamoms
1 inch (2.5 cm) cassia bark
3 whole cloves

SPICES 2
1 teaspoon ground coriander
1 teaspoon ground white cummin

Cut the chicken into 1 inch (2.5 cm) cubes.

Blend the nuts, ginger, garlic and chillies and yoghurt into a stiff coarse paste.

Heat the oil and fry SPICES 1 for 5 minutes. Add the onion and fry for a further 5 minutes. Add SPICES 2 and cook for 5 more minutes.

Preheat oven to 190°C/375°F/Gas 5.

Combine the paste, spiced purée and chicken in a casserole dish and mix well. Cook in the oven for 35–40 minutes. (Stir halfway through, adding a little water if needed.) Add the cream and salt to taste, then cook for a further 15 minutes.

Sprinkle on the fresh coriander or parsley and serve.

Serves 4

'All actions stem from food.'

'Food must be worshipped for it enhances the faculties.'

'Through food comes the end of ignorance and bondage.'

From the Rig-Veda, the holy writings of the Hindus written between 1500 and 800 BC

TANDOORI CHICKEN

To make authentic tandoori you need a special clay oven, but for this recipe an ordinary barbecue set or a regular gas or electric oven and grill will do. The secrets of tasty tandoori include a colourful marinade of spices in yoghurt and a short sharp baking. This baked spicy chicken dish is equally successful with duck, quail, pigeon, rabbit and lobster. Serve with nan bread, lettuce, lemon wedges, and mint chutney.

4 large chicken breasts or legs
3 tablespoons lime or lemon juice
1 teaspoon salt

MARINADE
5 fl oz (150 ml) yoghurt
2 tablespoons mustard oil
1 tablespoon garlic purée (see page 33)
1 teaspoon salt

MARINADE SPICES
1½ teaspoons ground coriander
1½ teaspoons ground cummin
1 teaspoon ground ginger
1½ teaspoons paprika
¼ teaspoon orange food colouring powder (optional)

Skin the chicken, then quarter it and slash the flesh with short gashes. Rub in the lime or lemon juice and the salt. Leave for 30 minutes or so.

Meanwhile, mix together all the marinade ingredients, including the SPICES. Rub thoroughly into the chicken (by hand is messy but best), and leave to stand in a covered bowl overnight.

Next day, preheat the oven to 210°C/425°F/Gas 7. Shake the excess marinade off the chicken pieces and place on oven racks. Make sure you put a drip pan underneath, preferably lined with aluminium foil. Cook for 25–30 minutes, then, to finish off, place under the grill for 3–4 minutes.

Alternatively, you can use the barbecue. Put the pieces of marinated chicken over the charcoal (not too near) and cook for about 30 minutes until tender.

Serves 4

CHINESE CURRY

Curry-eating may not be prevalent in China, but an interesting variation on the curry theme appears in Chinese restaurants. This curry is light in texture, slightly sweet and a pleasant golden brown colour. The duck and orange combination works well, but don't be afraid to use pork, prawns or vegetables in place of the duck.

1½ lb (680 g) duck meat (see method)
3 tablespoons vegetable oil
2 tablespoons cornflour
5 fl oz (150 ml) onion purée (see page 33)
1 tablespoon tomato purée
1 tablespoon green capsicum, chopped
1 tablespoon red capsicum, chopped
1 small tin mandarin oranges/tangerines (up to
    10½ oz/298 g)
Salt
Brown sugar

SPICES 1
1 inch (2.5 cm) piece cassia bark
3 cloves
1 teaspoon coriander seeds
½ teaspoon cummin seeds
2 teaspoons fennel seeds
2 star anise

SPICES 2
½ teaspoon white pepper
1 teaspoon turmeric

Because duck is rather oily, it is a good idea to part-roast it first for about half an hour in the oven. Keep the dripping. When cool, cut up the duck either on or off the bone.

Grind SPICES 1 to a fine powder. Add in SPICES 2.

In a pan (preferably a wok) mix the oil and corn-flour and heat, stirring until it is well mixed. Add the spices, continue stirring and cook for a couple of minutes.

Slowly add a cupful of water while stirring – keep adding water until you get a good thick 'creamy' texture, and it stops thickening.

At this point, add the onion purée, tomato purée, green and red capsicums, the orange pieces and juice, and stir-fry for 5 minutes. Add salt and sugar to taste.

Add the duck and simmer for 10–15 minutes until well cooked. Add extra water if necessary.

Serves 4

THAI CURRY

Thai curries are zesty and spicy. Specialist ingredients include peanuts and lemon grass, as in this delicious but hot beef curry.

1½ lb (680 g) lean beef
4–5 tablespoons vegetable oil
8 fl oz (200 ml) onion purée (see page 33)
3 tablespoons garlic purée (see page 33)
2 oz (50 g) desiccated coconut
3 oz (75 g) peanuts (raw, unsalted)
2 blades lemon grass, fresh or dried, chopped
1 teaspoon anchovy essence
6 green chillis, chopped
Salt

SPICES 1
¼ teaspoon asafoetida
1 teaspoon ground coriander
1 teaspoon ground cummin
1 teaspoon mango powder
1 teaspoon ground black pepper
1 teaspoon turmeric

SPICES 2
4 green cardamoms
2 inch (5 cm) piece cassia bark

Fry the beef in the oil for 10 minutes. Lift to a plate and reserve the oil. Fry the purées in the oil for 10 minutes.

Make a paste of SPICES 1 using a little water and add the paste to the purée and fry for a further 5 minutes.

Combine the meat and remaining ingredients including SPICES 2 but excluding the salt, in a casserole. Place in an oven preheated to 190°C/375°F/Gas 5, and cook for 45 minutes. Add salt to taste and serve.

Serves 4

THINGS WHICH GO WITH CURRY

RICE

Rice is the staple food of over half the world's population. The types used in curry cooking are long-grained, which are not too glutinous. The notable types are Patna and Basmati. The latter has a superb fragrance and texture, and grows from the Himalayas to the southern-most tip of Sri Lanka.

When the plant is cropped, it is dried in the sun, then threshed to separate the rice grains. The inedible husk is removed and the remaining grain, at this stage known as paddy or brown rice, retains most of its nutrients – protein, fibre, carbohydrates and Vitamin B_1. Polishing cleans the rice but removes some of the nutrients. Recent techniques have produced an 'instant cook' rice which has all its goodness polished away, and to make matters worse is coated with chemicals to prevent oxidation. Good quality rice is not over-polished; but it should be inspected to ensure grit and dirt are removed, and rinsed to remove the dust.

2 pints (a generous litre) water
12 oz (350 g) Basmati or other long-grained rice
Salt

Boil the water, add the rice and a little salt and start timing. It takes 8–10 minutes. Stir frequently. As soon as the centre is no longer brittle, but still has a good 'bite' to it, strain off the water. The rice should be slightly under-cooked.

Place the strainer under the cold tap and cool the rice down to prevent further cooking. Shake off all excess water. Tip the rice into a serving dish and put in a low oven or warming drawer for about 30 minutes. As it dries and warms through, the grains will separate and become fluffy.

Serves 4–6

CHUPATTI

There are several forms of Indian bread and the *chupatti* is probably the best known. It is a flat circular disc of about 6 inches (15 cm) made from wheat and simply griddled.

8 oz (225 g) ata or wholemeal flour
About 2–4 tablespoons water

Mix flour in a bowl with sufficient water to make a dough which leaves the sides of the bowl clean. Take the dough out of the bowl and knead for a few minutes, then divide into 4 equal pieces and roll each one out quite thickly to about 6 inches (15 cm) in diameter.

Heat a frying pan to very hot. Test it by flicking a tiny bit of flour on the bottom of the pan. If it turns brown at once the pan is ready.

Using no oil, cook a chupatti on one side only. Using a spatula or fish slice, take the chupatti out of the pan and place it, uncooked side up, under a pre-heated grill. The top side will now cook and should puff up. Serve and eat immediately, and prepare the other chupattis similarly.

TARKA DHAL

Lentils are extremely nutritious but they are notoriously difficult to digest, and when cooked as dhals, they usually have spices such as asafoetida added which counter flatulence. For a truly economic and delicious supper, serve a simple meal consisting only of dhal and rice.

2 oz (50 g) polished red lentils
12 fl oz (350 ml) water
2 tablespoons ghee or oil
2 tablespoons onion purée (see page 33)
2 teaspoons garlic purée (see page 33)
1 small onion, sliced into long thin strips (optional)
Salt to taste

SPICES
1 teaspoon cummin seeds
½ teaspoon black peppercorns (optional)
¼ teaspoon asafoetida
½ teaspoon turmeric

Sift through the lentils to remove grit, etc., then wash them and soak them for 1 hour.

Boil the water, then add the lentils. Stir well, and cook for about 30 minutes, stirring from time to time and adding a little more water if needed.

Meanwhile fry the cummin and peppercorns for 2 minutes, then add the purées, asafoetida and turmeric and fry for 5 more minutes. Add the sliced onion and spice and purée mixture to the lentils when they are cooked, plus salt to taste.

Serve immediately or put into a warming drawer or low oven where it will keep quite happily. If you have time, fry an onion garnish for the dhal.

Serves 4

CHUTNEYS AND PICKLES

Chutneys are usually made from vegetables such as onion, cucumber, capsicum, fennel, lettuce and raddish, which are shredded or chopped and lightly spiced, with perhaps a twist of lemon to provide a fresh or sharp counter to the rich curry.

Pickles are more elaborate, involving the cooking of vegetables, meat or seafood in spices and oil. Usually they undergo a period of marination in vats or bottles in the Indian sun for anything from two weeks to two years before they are eaten. They keep indefinitely.

Yoghurt is used extensively as a chutney, either plain or with spices and all types of vegetables.

THE INDIAN MENU

MILD CURRIES

Korma: The mildest. Its colour can range from white to pale yellow, but it should contain nuts and cream.

Bhoona: A mild curry which should be quite dry.

MEDIUM STRENGTH CURRIES

Ceylon: Usually cooked with coconut, lemon and green capsicum. A hot version may include green chillies.

Dhansak: The curry base includes puréed lentils and aubergine.

Do-piaza: This one has a lot of cooked onion.

Jal Frezi: Contains dryish curried meat, cooked onion slices and green and red capsicum.

Kashmiri: Should be quite aromatic with almonds, and sometimes lotus roots or lychees.

Keema: Minced meat curry.

Makhanwalla or Makhani: Usually chicken, baked tandoori-style, then cooked in a sauce of cream and tomato.

Methi Gosht: A savoury curry in which the principal ingredient is cooked in fenugreek leaves.

Pasanda: Thin slices of curried meat.

Patia: A sweet and sour curry, normally seafood.

Rhogan Gosht: Aromatic and creamy, being cooked in yoghurt and tomato. Originally lamb, though restaurants do sometimes offer chicken or seafood variants.

Sag Gosht: The principal ingredient is cooked in spinach purée.

HOT CURRIES

Madras: The principal ingredient is cooked in a curry containing tomato purée and ground almonds.

Vindaloo: Hotter than Madras and, in the restaurant, usually lacking subtlety.

Tindaloo or Bindaloo or Bangalore: Hotter than Vindaloo.

Phal: The hottest curry the restaurant can offer.

THE INDIAN MEAL

A simple meal in India could well consist of just one curry, with plain boiled rice and one fresh chutney. For a more elaborate occasion, the meal could include two, three or even more curries, plus rice, dhal, bread and several chutneys. At an Indian celebration, such as a wedding, there seems to be no end to the array of dishes on offer. On such an occasion the diners usually help themselves to the selection of their choice. The great fun in cooking Indian food lies in the selection of dishes, and for that reason curry is perfect for parties.

KEEPING CURRY

Curries can be cooked a day or two in advance and stored in the refrigerator. The taste and texture will change slightly as the food marinates, but it will not be harmed. Curries keep in the freezer, but the larger aromatic spices are better removed beforehand as they tend to gain in strength and become a little powerful. Rice freezes, but it is never as good as fresh. It does, however, keep for a day without any serious deterioration.

SERVING

There are many ways of serving curry in India. In the richest homes the curries and the 'sundries' are placed in a number of small round bowls which come to the diner on a tray called *thali*. In the south, a fresh banana leaf is used as a disposable plate.

In many homes the food is eaten with the fingers. It is clean, efficient and cheap – and requires considerable skill. It saves on the washing up, too! In middle-class India, as over here, plates and cutlery are preferred.

The meal is best brought to the table piping hot in serving bowls. The diners can then help themselves.

DRINK

Some people drink nothing but water with a curry; others say water causes one to bloat and should be avoided at all costs. Mineral water is very acceptable, as are squashes, especially if fresh. Light beer or lager is popular with curry, both here and in India. There is hot debate about wine: many food writers decry the use of wine with curry, saying that the 'hot' spices ruin the delicate flavour of the wine. The argument wears a bit thin if you are drinking cheap 'plonk', when the wine may ruin the delicate spicing of a dish like korma. There is at least one top Indian restaurant in London where Chateau Latour is on the menu. If you enjoy wine, there is no good reason why you should not enjoy it with curry. And if you are feeling extravagant – try champagne.

THE CURRY CLUB

A very useful facility for those who like curry is The Curry Club, founded in 1982 by Pat Chapman. Its function is to bring together every piece of intelligence about curry in a useful, informative and entertaining way. It produces magazines, a guide to restaurants and a range of handy spice mix packs. The Club puts on gourmet curry evenings and 'club nights', and organises club gourmet holidays to the curry lands. For those who find it hard or inconvenient to get the special ingredients there is a handy mail-order service and in 1985 the Club opened its first retail shop in London's prestigious Covent Garden.

Pat Chapman has written a full-size book on curries – *The Curry Club Indian Restaurant Cookbook,* also published by Piatkus. It contains a 35-page introduction to curry-making and over 150 recipes.